_____GUIDE_____

TO

Memorizing Music

By

A. J. GOODRICH,

AUTHOR OF

Complete Music Analysis,

Analytical Harmony,

Synthetic Counterpoint,

Theory of Interpretation,

Music as a Language,

The Art of Song, Etc.

Windham Press is committed to bringing the lost cultural heritage of ages past into the 21st century through high-quality reproductions of original, classic printed works at affordable prices.

This book has been carefully crafted to utilize the original images of antique books rather than error-prone OCR text. This also preserves the work of the original typesetters of these classics, unknown craftsmen who laid out the text, often by hand, of each and every page you will read. Their subtle art involving judgment and interaction with the text is in many ways superior and more human than the mechanical methods utilized today, and gave each book a unique, hand-crafted feel in its text that connected the reader organically to the art of bindery and book-making.

We think these benefits are worth the occasional imperfection resulting from the age of these books at the time of scanning, and their vintage feel provides a connection to the past that goes beyond the mere words of the text.

As bibliophiles, we are always seeking perfection in our work, so please notify us of any errors in this book by emailing us at corrections@windhampress.com. Our team is motivated to correct errors quickly so future customers are better served. Our mission is to raise the bar of quality for reprinted works by a focus on detail and quality over mass production.

To peruse our catalog of carefully curated classic works, please visit our online store at www.windhampress.com.

WINDHAM PRESS
CLASSIC REPRINTS

PREFACE.

The sub-title to this volume might lead certain readers to infer that memorizing is entirely ignored. Such is not the case. What the author is warring against is, the customary mechanical process of memorizing by rote—*i. e.*, playing the notes and repeating them until they are remembered, but without attempting to penetrate the design of the composer. It is very difficult, and frequently impossible, to remember music that has not been mentally assimilated. Memory must be aided by some form of impression, or sensorial effect, or by the application of an inherent principle which will tend to reveal the design and structure of the music to be learned.

"Events that excite little attention," says Webster, "are apt to escape from memory." Hence the rote process not only requires more time for its accomplishment, but its tenure is very insecure.

Nearly everyone must be aware of the fact that it is much easier to remember the face than the name of a newly formed acquaintance. If we are in the habit of observing facial outline and expression we will unconsciously note some peculiarity which is plainly recognizable under ordinary circumstances. The result of our observation will be a sensorial impression more or less indelible. Thus the face would be remembered long after the name had been forgotten, even though we repeated the latter and made an effort "to commit it to memory." Unless the name were very unique, or already familiar to us, there would be nothing in it to aid the memory in its reminiscent endeavors.

These psychologic principles are directly applicable to music.

.   The author has endeavored in this presentment to illustrate the various means by which intelligent students may in a comparatively short space of time become possessed of any musical composition suited to their technical equipment.

The result is three-fold :

1. There is a great economizing of time.

2. The music thus acquired is more thoroughly understood.

3. It is more securely retained by the power of memory.

The author confidently asserts that many compositions can be learned according to this system in one-half (and some in one-fourth) of the time usually required.

As one may breathe correctly and sing excellently without knowing whether the diaphragm is an active or a passive muscle, so it seems unnecessary to enter into an elaborate dissertation upon the different agencies employed in effecting this result. They are merely mentioned here, in miscellaneous order: 1. Familiarity with the elemental material of music—scales and chords, measure and rhythm. 2. The principles of harmonic progression, etc. 3. Analysis of the musical design. 4. The continuation or enlargement of this design according to the same general principles which governed the composer. 5. Conventional outlines of form which tend to reveal the order and tonality of different divisions and subdivisions in certain styles of music.

This system is not based upon the various "forms of memory" enumerated by metaphysical writers. In truth the student is neither asked nor expected to "memorize" pages of printed music, nor even a single paragraph of the text. The author has observed so many detrimental results from the prevailing methods of memorizing that he almost entirely eliminated that word from the original text.

"Finger memory" is but a name for whatever the hands have been trained in advance to execute. If a difficult figure has been mastered in one of Cramer's or Clementi's etudes, and we encounter that same figure in a sonata by Beethoven, the original difficulty will no longer exist. That is an important assistant, but it is only technical. The fingers may acquire a muscular habit of performing certain feats and evolutions, but the fingers have no "memory." What we remember from having seen is called "visual memory;" what we remember from having heard is termed "auricular memory." When the understanding is especially involved (and in learning music it always should be) that is an example of "intellectual memory." But memory in any form is essentially an intellectual faculty, whether it be operated upon by the visual, auricular, olfactory or other senses.

In music the principal secret to rapid mastery of a given passage consists in *apprehending the design.* We must be able to hear it internally and analyze all its phases. We then possess it mentally. The extended scale passage at the close of Chopin's Scherzo, Op. 54, will serve as an illustration of one of the many time-saving means to be employed. The scale begins at the lowest *E* and ascends to the highest. Soon as the rhythmic arrangement is observed the entire passage can be played *sans* notes and without committing the latter to memory. It is unnecessary to read every note ; the experienced pianist sees at a glance that the scale of *E* is continued from the lowest to the highest *E* on a modern piano. These extreme points form the exterior lines ; any one who knows the scales can supply the detail. All such designs, if properly understood, will produce an impression and thus obviate the seeming necessity for repeating the passage many times until it is "memorized." There is as little reason for reading every note as there is for spelling every word in the perusal of a book.

As mental discipline and incentive to rapid thought no other study is so valuable as is this system of apprehending and executing musical designs, thus re-creating the composer's transcript.

A. J. GOODRICH.

New York, *May, 1906.*

CONTENTS.

8   *Contents.*

LESSON I.

DIATONIC MELODIC SEQUENCES.

MOTIVE—DESIGN.

The major portion of this system is based upon melodic and harmonic sequences in some of their forms. Repetition, and sequence (which is a species of altered repetition), enter so prominently into the structure of music that whoever understands the principles and applications of these elements possesses the key which will unlock almost every investiture of notes.

In order to master a composition quickly it is essential that the performer shall be able to reproduce a considerable portion of the music by means of sequence, repetition or other methods for continuing and enlarging a motive.

We will presuppose that a given page of music consists of a motive or group continued in sequence through various tonalities—such frequently being the case. Soon as the design is apprehended an expert performer ought to be able to play the page correctly without further reference to the notes. After repeating it slowly two or three times the actual notes would be learned, without having resorted to the usual, tedious process of "memorizing" them. To increase the movement gradually and to include the proper style of performance would be matters of technic and taste. With these subjects the present system has little to do.

SEQUENCE.

If the motive is *a*, *b*, *c*, the sequence will be *b*, *c*, *d*, ascending, or *g*, *a*, *b*, descending. The word Sequence is, therefore, to be understood in its literal sense, *i. e.*, "the order of following." The various forms of sequence will be illustrated and applied in their proper order.

At present all the sequences will be diatonic and free. Hence they are to be continued according to the key in which they occur. All that is presupposed is this: that the student understands all the major and minor scales, with their common chords, and can write or play them readily. Without this foundation to build upon, no satisfactory progress can be made with this, or any other rational system. It is not sufficient to copy the scales from a book, nor to play them by note. (They ought never to be written in an instruction book.) All the major scales are theoretically identical; therefore the formula for the *C* scale is sufficient, if this formula is transferred to any given pitch. The same simple theory applies to melodic and harmonic minor scales, and to the common chords of both modes.

A short diatonic motive (the first three notes of Schubert's great *C major* Symphony) is selected. *Do not begin by playing this motive*, but by *examining it carefully*. Consider that from this germ the composer evolves an entire music structure, and that we must understand the ordinary methods of construction followed by the composer in order to re-create even a part of his music. (The usual process of "committing the notes to memory" is not to be employed in this system.) Here is the motive:

Ex. 1.

Every point and feature is to be observed, and this preliminary information is to be elicited in some such manner as the following: 1. What clef sign is used? 2. What is the key? (Every signature may represent a major or its relative minor.) 3. What is the measure signature? 4. Upon what tone of the key does the motive begin? 5. Describe the motive melodically. (Is it a scale or chord figure? does it go up or down, and how far?) 6. Describe it rhythmically. (What is the value of the notes? do they fill an entire measure, or only part of a measure?) 7. Count it, according to the mensural signature.

When the facts are understood that the motive begins upon the tonic of *C*, and ascends scalewise to the third of the key, two counts to the first note and one count to each of the following notes, the student will have a sufficient nucleus for the next step.

The motive is to be repeated upon successive degrees of the scale, each sequence to begin upon the note next above the beginning of the preceding figure. Accordingly the following would not be a regular sequence:

The second measure in Ex. 3 may be considered as a sequence, but it is not sufficiently elementary:

The altered rhythm, also, is unusual in sequence and involves a principle which cannot be considered here.

Another form results from repeating the last note of each motive group, thus:

This approaches a little nearer to the desired formula, and will appear later. But the most simple and natural sequence will represent a scale melody, the outline of which contains the following accented notes:

Ascending.

Ex. 5.

The delineation naturally follows the outline.

The student may now proceed slowly to execute the design, which consists of a short period in sequence form. Keep in mind the motive, and repeat this upon every tone of the scale, thus:

Ex. 6. *Andante.*

Every motive group ascends a third, scalewise.

Measures 7 and 8 have the effect of an authentic cadence, which is of course appropriate to the end of a period.

If any errors are committed (they are generally inexcusable) do not attempt to correct them at the time, but proceed undisturbed with the regular slow movement. Then repeat the entire exercise more carefully.

Now continue the transpositions in the following keys: *D, E flat, E, F, F sharp* (or *G flat*), *G, A flat, B flat* and *B.* The measure may be changed to this:

Ex. 7.

As the design becomes more familiar the movement is to be increased until it can be played *allegro* and without a mistake. Before any of the designs are played rapidly the fingering should be determined upon according to well known methods.

The same motive is to be played in a descending movement, with the scale as an outline, as suggested:

(a.)

Ex. 8.

The cadence may be slightly altered :

Ex. 8 also is to be transposed.

It is important that the melodic principle, illustrated in Ex. 6, be well understood, since it finds such frequent application in the best music. This appears even in fundamental progressions, as thus :

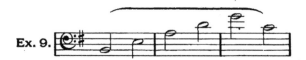

Ex. 9.

This would be very inconvenient, if not impossible, to the singer, and moreover the melodic outline is sacrificed. The student may rearrange this passage, and in such manner as to indicate a scale melody on the main accents. Begin on the same note; in fact, the first measure is not to be altered, but the compass of the passage is to be greatly curtailed and condensed.

Ex. 10 is for the left hand. Analyze it in the same manner. Observe particularly the nature of the figure and the degree of the scale upon which it begins:

Ex. 10.

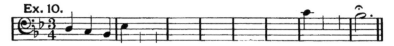

Transpose without notes to *B, C, D flat, D, E flat, E, F, F sharp, G, A flat* and *A.*

The next step consists in combining the motives 7 and 10, for both hands. The latter is the same as the former, in reverse order, and the two form a simple subject and countersubject. In other words, 10 is a contrary inversion of 7.

Continue the two parts melodically. The movements are all contrary :

(a.)

Ex. 11.  etc.

Notwithstanding the fact that the left hand part skips a fourth, as shown by the /, the sequence is perfectly regular. Every group begins a diatonic tone higher. This rather than the skip of a fourth, should be borne in mind, while the duet is being performed. The outline of the left hand part is therefore equally melodious : *D, E flat, F, G, A, B flat, C.* The two parts end upon the octave—tonic above and below.

Transpose into. several other major keys. In every instance play the parts separately at first.

The motive should now be inverted, (a) below, and (b) above :

Ex. 12.  etc.

Continue as usual, eight measures, to a cadence on *A flat.* Then transpose.

Another simple motive is quoted, and this also is to be continued by means of sequence :

CORELLI.

Ex. 13.  etc.

(descending.)

Proceed to analyze the motive soon as it appears. This last begins on the third of *D major*, ascends a fourth and descends a second, diatonically.* Each succeeding figure begins on the tone below. The outline will, therefore, be a scale melody, as in the previous examples. Continue six measures to a cadence on *D.*

---

* Diatonic refers to the natural tones in a key, major or minor.

The next step consists in adding a single part for the left hand in this rhythm : | ♩ ꞌ ♩ ꞌ | a third below the first note of each upper group.

When this scheme is sufficiently understood, transpose the two parts into *E flat*, *E*, *F*, *F sharp and G*.

Now invert the parts in an ascending movement, thus :

Ex. 14.  etc.

The attention is to be concentrated principally upon the left hand figures, the right hand part being very simple. The melodic outlines and the skip of a fourth claim constant attention and quick perception.

NOTE.—The mistakes which occur in following this system are due either to carelessness, or want of mental application. Hence it is important that the pupil shall acquire the habit of analyzing every motive and design intelligently, and proceeding slowly. Every group or figure should present to the mind a musical image. One will soon acquire the art of hearing mentally each motive, if the motive is always examined attentively before its execution is attempted.

It is not so much the actual notes, as it is the *intervals*, that are to be impressed upon the mind. These admit of free transposition, whereas the mere notes do not. The former is a mere parrot-like process of repeating from memory ; the latter is a theory which at once calls into action the mental forces.

We may not long remember that our friend lives in the house numbered 3468 Walnut Street, because there is nothing to assist the memory in retaining those figures. But if we have observed the form or style of the house, the curving footpath strewn with shells, a peculiar rosebush, or any characteristic detail which produced an actual impression upon us, we remember it without effort, and the remembrance remains with us almost indefinitely.

LESSON II.

MELODIC SEQUENCE CONTINUED.

A motive for the left hand is here presented. Observe the key, the mensural signature, and particularly the intervals:

(a.)

Ex. 15.

Beginning upon the tonic, the intervals are, a third below and a second above. The last note of one group becomes the first of the next group. The sequence then proceeds according to the scale of this key. Play slowly and repeat; then increase the movement.

Number 13 in the right hand and 15 in the left hand are now to be united. This is not so easy; but if each motive is well understood, the two can be combined without difficulty, thus:

(b.)

etc.

Play slow and repeat. Transpose to *E flat, E, F, F sharp, G, and A flat.*

A motive figure of four notes is next in order :

LISZT.

Ex. 16.

Proceed at once, before attempting to sound this motive, to analyze it. Observe the treble staff; the tonal and mensural signature; the intervals; the starting point and the rhythm. (In free sequence it is sufficient to recognize the intervals numerically.) As the motive is observed and mentally noted, endeavor to *hear the effect*, at least approximately. The figures may now be continued in ascending sequence form, ending upon the upper key-tone.

Transpose Ex. 16 to *E, F, F sharp, G, and A flat.* Keep constantly in mind the intervalic formula—up a third, up a fifth, and down a second, major or minor, according to the key. Also play the motive descending with the left hand.

The group from Liszt may then be taken inversely : down a third, down a fifth, and up a second. One must learn to think of the intervals quickly and accurately from every part of the scale. The greater the distance of the interval the more difficulty will be experienced in computing it quickly. The eye must be trained to distinguish at a glance the appearance of thirds, fourths, fifths, sixths, sevenths and octaves, as they appear in print, and their corresponding keys on an instrument. Perhaps the better way for elementary pupils will be to play a series of thirds ascending and descending an octave or more ; then fourths, fifths, and so on. This form may be used :

Ex. 17.

A few examples are to be written by the pupil ; then put away the notes and play what has been written.

Do not attempt to play the fourths and fifths in this form :

Ex. 18.

But preserve a melodic outline, thus :

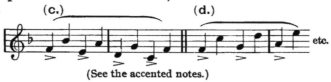

(See the accented notes.)

At (c) the ascending fourth and descending fifth are synonymous. The sequence at (d) is to be understood in the same way. A sequence of fourths may also be represented

by the interval formula—up a fourth, down a third, and up a
fourth.   In notation, thus :

The next example introduces a different kind of sequence.
It is intended to repeat each group a third below, as in the
finale to Beethoven's Op. 31, I.   The motive has already
been given, and therefore the next step is comparatively
simple.   The first group is to be played by the right hand.
This is repeated a third lower by the left hand.   The third
group falls to the right hand, the fourth to the left hand, and
so on.   An outline is given :

After repeating this, begin an octave higher and continue
the sequence in the same manner four octaves lower.   The
cadence should fall upon the key-tone.   Then transpose into
other keys until the entire passage can be played accurately,
at the rate of (♩ = 120.)

Following is a contrary inversion (*per moto contrario*) of
Ex. 16 :

Perhaps this has already been accomplished.   If not,
observe all the features previously mentioned and proceed
with the sequence.

A group of six notes forms the next motive.

The simplest analysis of this is, to consider the last four notes as a turn on the tonic, or root-note of the chord. Therefore there is a third, a fifth, and a turn beginning on the highest note. The outline is :

or, plainer still,

There is to be a measured gruppetto on each upper note. To a musician this harmonic view is much simpler, because it is suggestive and enables him to carry out the design with perfect surety. Therefore the students would better acquire this mode of analysis, even though it may not at first seem as plain as the melodic analysis previously employed. Continue the ascending movement one or two octaves, then transpose.

The next exercise is for the left hand:

After analyzing the intervals melodically and observing the rhythm, continue to

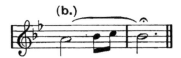

Repeat two or three times.

Examples 21 (a) and 22 (a) are to be combined for both hands. Before commencing, make a mental note of each figure. The upper part, being less simple, will require more attention. Both figures (above and below) begin a note higher in each succeeding measure; and they start a third apart. Therefore this outline must be apprehended instantly as the sequence progresses :

Proceed slowly and increase the movement gradually; then transpose.

NOTA BENE.—Success in this, as in other important matters, depends so greatly upon the performer's ability to think clearly and quickly that the author cannot contain himself with a mere presentation of the material to be developed, however much care he may bestow upon the systemizing of the examples. To evoke and direct thought should be the principal aim of education, but alas! the intellectual functions are usually allowed to remain dormant, and if a spark of thought chance to germinate, it is smothered with incongruous fuel. These "cramming" methods cannot be applied to this system, nor to the proper study of any branch of music. The mind of the musician, above all others, must act instantaneously. Therefore cultivate the art of thinking quickly and accurately. Select a phrase from some master and examine it attentively and patiently until it reveals at least one point of information unknown before. For instance, this phrase :

"Album Leaf." GADE.

Ex. 23.

In this excerpt there is considerable to be discovered, yet it is quite simple. Careful examination and comparison will surely yield their reward.

Several clews have been given as to the mental processes involved in apprehending a music design. These must invariably be employed until they operate without effort—almost automatically.

A variant of the motive 21, here follows :

There are two diatonic thirds, a second, and then a gruppetto beginning upon the note above. It is plainly an embellishment of the common triad in its second close position :

The sequence should be composed mentally by imagining the notes as they would be written in continuing the design, thus : *F, A, C* (or *C sharp*), *D, E, D, C, D*, and so on.

By means of thinking out the problem, *away from the keyboard*, the actual performance of the passage becomes a simple matter, because the pupil will then know exactly what is to do.

Continue one or two octaves above, then transpose to *D flat, D, E flat, E and F.*

The last motive is now to be played inversely by the left hand. In this form it will fall quite naturally to the same fingers used in the right hand example, and in the same order : 1, 2, 3, 4, 5, 4, 3, 4.

Analyze this new figure in the same manner, and compose the sequence mentally before attempting its performance. The position of the hand is very nearly the same in each figure.

Transpose to other keys.

LESSON III.

HARMONIC CADENCES—MAJOR.

A sufficient number of melodic sequences for the present have been given, and now, before we can proceed with the harmonic sequences, the student must know the common fundamental harmonies in all keys, and be able to play them readily. This is imperative.*

The cadence harmonies consist, primarily, of three chords : The tonic (1) ; the subdominant (4) ; the dominant (5). These are well known ; but so few elementary and medium grade pupils can play chord progressions correctly that the author will here present a simple statement of the formula.

1. The student will name the notes which comprise the chord of the tonic—say in the key of *G*. (Mention the root-note first, the third next, and the fifth last.) 2. Mention in the same order the notes of the chord of the subdominant. 3. Mention the notes which comprise the dominant chord.

If correctly named, these notes will form the scale of *G*. Hence they must belong to the key of *G*.

Now begin with the tonic chord in its first close position, root in the base. The next chord is to be that of the subdominant. Is there a note in the *G* chord which occurs in the *C* chord? If so, this is a *connecting note*, and it is to be played, or held down, by the same finger in both chords. (This agrees with the principle used in writing chords—that a connecting note between two different harmonies remains in the same voice-part.)

If we begin with

Ex. 25.

---

* Those who are expert in key-board harmony may omit this lesson.

(22)

the connecting note will appear lowermost in both chords. This fixes the position of the *C* chord, because we know that the other two notes must be added above the tied note, *G.*

Now play both chords.

This progression from tonic (T) to subdominant (S) should be played in three close positions, thus :

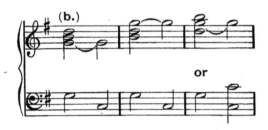

Observe particularly that the note of connection occurs first below, then at the top, and then in the middle. Practice this without notes.

When there is no connecting note between two chords the upper parts are to move in an opposite direction to that of the base, in order to prevent ungrammatical parallel progressions, thus :

Ex. 26.

This is wrong. Read again the directions in the preceding paragraph, and then correct the progression. The base will remain, but the *G* above must descend to *F sharp*.

When this is understood, play three arrangements according to the following outlines :

Add the roots in the left hand, and observe that the treble parts descend while the bass ascends a second.

The complete cadence is now in order. The formula is, tonic, sub-dominant, dominant and tonic.

Observe scrupulously the directions pertaining to connected and disconnected chord progressions. The melody and bass parts are given as outlines:

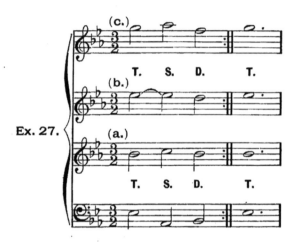

Ex. 27.

The chords are to be completed beneath each of these melodic phrases; (b) and (c) are the same, harmonically, as (a). If a clew is needed it is furnished by the score being read vertically, all the parts at once.

These cadences are essentially harmonic and serve as accompaniments to melodies. Therefore they should be played fundamentally (from the root basses) without particular regard to melody. And this somewhat simplifies the student's task. Practice the last cadence, and the one in *G*, until they can be performed in moderate tempo without hesitating, and without notes.

The complete harmonic cadence must be played in all the major keys; but in every instance there is a preliminary process to be accomplished in order to avoid errors: 1. Name tonic, sub-dominant and dominant in each new key. (Merely single out 1, 4 and 5, according to the scale.) 2. Name the chords of those three fundamentals. 3. Imagine the note common to the T. and S. 4. From S. to D. is a disconnected progression; hence one must think of the bass and treble parts as moving contrarily. It is well to play the fundamentals in the left hand slowly and think of each chord represented by the root-note in the bass. For instance, in *E*:

Ex. 28.

These root-notes should suggest the three major chords, *E*, *A*, and *B*. Then apply the principles of chord progression as explained and play the cadence in three close positions, same bass to each re-arrangement. See Ex. 27. Do not neglect any of this work, but become familiar with the cadence harmonies in *all keys*. Whatever time may be required to do this will be amply repaid in future work. In fact, this key-board knowledge of the cadences is *absolutely essential to success.*

Mistakes are unnecessary and therefore inexcusable. Hence, if errors occur, the student should understand that the directions have not been properly applied.

When the previous formula has been mastered the cadence may be varied in different ways. For instance, by using different positions of each chord as shown in the following:

Ex. 29.

Play the roots in the left hand in whole notes. The same principles apply here.

Repeat, then carry out the design in two other close positions, same bass.

Also transpose Ex. 29.

LESSON IV.

HARMONIC CADENCES—MINOR.

The fundamental basses to a complete cadence in minor are identical with those in tonic major. In *E* minor, for example, the bass would be : E, A, B, E, exactly as it was in Ex. 28, which see.

Before attempting the minor cadences the student is to play slowly the harmonic minor scale of *G*. The complete cadence will embrace every tone in this scale. This will serve to explain why the dominant is a major chord, though the tonic and sub-dominant are naturally minor in every minor key. The order in which the chords follow one another is the same in both modes, and the principles of chord progression also are the same. The fundamentals are indicated in the following example. Therefore the chords are to be, *G minor*, *C minor* and *D major*—according to the harmonic minor scale of *G* :

Ex. 30.

Each complete cadence is to be performed in three close positions. (See Ex. 27, a, b, c.)

Transpose to *G sharp* (or *A flat*) minor; play the scale first, then select 1, 4, 5, as the fundamentals for the left hand. Each bass note, being a root, represents the common chord of that note; *i. e.*, the root, third and fifth. See that the chords agree with the scale ; then the leading note (major third of the dominant chord) will not be omitted. Include three positions.

Continue the transposition through *A minor*, *B flat minor*,

B minor, *C minor*, *C sharp minor*, *D minor*, *E flat minor*, *E minor*, *F minor*, and *F sharp minor*.

In every instance the scale is to precede the cadence, and the chords must be imagined, or seen mentally, before they are played. Connecting notes (keys) remain stationary; when the chords are disconnected the right hand part moves in an opposite direction to that of the left hand.

Soon as this is fairly well understood and carried out on the key-board, the form may be varied, though the chords follow one another in the same order.

A few indications are given :

Ex. 31.

Include two more positions, same bass.

This ends upon the minor third ; the next re-arrangement will end upon the fifth ; the last re-arrangement will end upon the tonic. Practice this until it can be performed in any key accurately, about ($\downarrow$. = 60).

Hesitating, and repeating on account of wrong notes, are the worse kind of mistakes. As a rule, a wrong note can never be corrected, and those who try to do so always " make a bad matter worse," for they destroy the rhythm or the movement, and this is a much more serious error than the mere playing of a false note. Few listeners notice an occasional error of intonation, unless the player calls attention to it by repeating; whereas every one is annoyed by stuttering and wrong tempo. The author's advice is, play carefully (that is to say, *thoughtfully*) so that everything will be reasonably correct. Then, if some casual error occurs, pay not the slightest attention to it, but proceed with the strict movement.

Finally, the complete cadences in major and in minor should be played in arpeggio form.   The following may serve as a model:

Add root-notes in the left hand.   The arpeggio figures are extensions of the common chords.   A mere glance at such passages ought to be sufficient to reveal their design and structure.   Even this is quite ordinary and may with advantage be varied.

See Harmonic Cadences in Analytical Harmony.

LESSON V.

There are several kinds of complete cadence, all of which are very nearly synonymous. In a major key the relative minor of the sub-dominant is frequently substituted for the latter. As there are two tones in common between these harmonies the effect is similar in both instances. Usually the substituted chord appears in its first inversion (third in the bass) in order to maintain the bass formula, T, S, D, T. The next example shows the relationship between the sub-dominant chord and its relative minor, with their theoretical roots below:

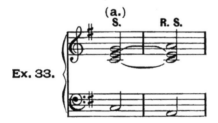

Ex. 33.

Example (b) illustrates the manner in which the relative minor of the sub-dominant (R. S.) is usually employed in harmonization:

BOHM.

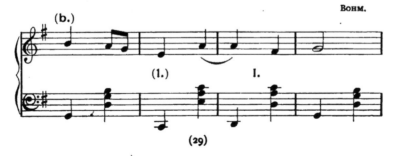

(29)

The symbol (1) is used in place of the old thorough-bass figures, $\frac{6}{3}$, to indicate the first inversion. The melody will usually suggest which chord (S. or R. S.) shall be employed in the accompaniment. (The Roman numeral, I, is the author's symbol for a dominant seventh, the first and most important discord encountered in the study of harmony.)

Ex. 33 (b), or the following, may be taken as a model for transposing:

Ex. 34.

The minor seventh is frequently added to the dominant chord in a complete cadence. The duplicated root of the sub-dominant chord remains as a connecting link, and becomes the seventh of the dominating harmony.

Ex. 35.

The fifth of the sub-dominant chord must not ascend to the fifth of the dominant chord, because that would produce parallel fifths with the bass. Accordingly two upper parts descend (as in Exs. 27 and 29), while the upper root-note of the sub-dominant chord remains and forms the seventh, like a suspension. The fifth of the dominant seventh harmony is omitted, but that is usually unimportant in such instances.

Two improper progressions are included in the next Example, because these errors (resulting from ignorance or carelessness) are frequently committed. Correct the progressions marked + :

Since these exercises are principally harmonic, the melody notes may be changed. (See Ex. 35, a.)

The following exercise is recommended for practice. Every three-measure phrase (excepting the last) ends with a dominant seventh chord in some related key. And in each instance the discord known as the dominant seventh is preceded by the sub-dominant to the new key. This latter chord, whether major or minor, is always a major second (" whole step ") below the root of the dominant seventh chord:

Ex. 36.

The fifth is omitted from every dominant seventh chord here.

Transpose to *D, E,* and *F sharp.*

Ex. 37 is similar, beginning and ending in minor. The formula is the same, so is the theory of chord progression:

Ex. 37.

Transpose to *A minor, B minor, C sharp minor,* and *F minor.* Practice the exercise until it can be played in regular movement, moderato.

Examples 33 and 34 must be modified when they are transposed from major to minor, because the sub-dominant to a minor key has no relative minor. But composers use as a substitute the imperfect triad founded a small third below the sub-dominant, as there are two notes in common:

Compare this with Ex. 33 (a) in *G major*.

See the last twenty-one measures, first allegro of Beethoven's Op. 2, I; the repeated scale passage accompanied by a kind of ground-bass. Also the andante to Beethoven's Sonatina in *G minor*, Op. 49, I; measures 7 and 12.

The sub-dominant and the imperfect triad are sometimes combined as a mixed sub-dominant harmony, thus:

Ex. 39.

This combination usually appears in its first inversion, as here. Transpose this into several other minor keys.

In like manner the sub-dominant chord and its relative minor are frequently combined in a major key. The example explains the entire *modus operandi*:

Ex. 40.

Measures (a) and (b) show the two sub-dominant harmonies. At (c) they are combined into a secondary discord (IV); (d) shows the application in music. Measure (e) is nearly the same, but more ponderous.

It will suffice to examine the last example carefully and then play it as written.

A more extended formula is given, and this is to be com_
pleted by the student :

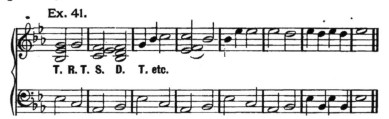

Ex. 41.

T. R. T. S. D. T. etc.

The second chord (R. T.) is, of course, the relative minor
of the tonic. Add the harmony to the last section in the same
manner. When the period is well under control transpose it
to *F, G, A,* and *B.*

PERFECT CADENCE.

This includes the previous chords, with the addition of
the second inversion of the tonic chord after the sub-dominant
and before the dominant. The bass has the fifth of the key
for the inverted chord and also for the dominant chord which
follows. The first is called a "real-bass" (marked $^6_4$ in the
thorough-bass books) ; the second is a fundamental, or root-
bass, thus :

Ex. 42.

The fourth above *d* is *g ;* the sixth is *b ;* but these may
be played in any of the following positions, according to
circumstances :

(b.)

The (2) below means that the bass note is fifth of the chord.   This is used by the author in place of the obsolete figures, ⁶₄.

Now play the perfect cadence in three close positions from the following bass part, as formula :

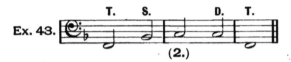

Here there is a connecting note throughout.   Imagine all the chords that are to be sounded before attempting to play the cadence.

Transpose to *F sharp, A flat, B flat, C,* and *D.*

A countless number of compositions are founded upon these simple cadence harmonies.   When the student is familiar with them in all keys it will be found that the harmonic basis of such *morceaux* as Weber's *Rondo brillante* is already known and ready to be applied.   Therefore the principal remaining task will consist in learning the themes, and observing the particular style of accompaniment intended by the composer.

LESSON VI.

THEMES AND DESIGNS FOUNDED UPON CADENCE HARMONIES.

The following excerpt from a modern sonatina illustrates
the practical application of the perfect cadence. Analyze the
melodic section carefully and endeavor to hear the accompanying harmony. Then play it without notes:

REINECKE.

The accompaniment is in plain chords with this rhythm:
(✗ ♩ ♩), except the close, which is (♩ ♩).

It is evident that such pieces are already more than half
learned (the theme is the lesser half), provided the pupil has
mastered the harmonic cadences in Lessons III, IV, and V.

Ex. 45 is in minor ; the imperfect triad being required in
place of the regular sub-dominant :

The harmonization and style of accompaniment are left to
the taste of the performer.

Transpose to several other minor keys.

We will now attempt to construct, according to the preceding principles, a short movement consisting of twenty
measures.

The first phrase is quoted :

Ex. 46.

(36)

This is a unison passage, the left hand having the same notes an octave lower.

The second phrase is to be accompanied by the perfect cadence formula. The melody is this :

The imperfect triad (mis-called " diminished ") was used by the composer in place of the sub-dominant, though the notes *d, e, f,* do not exclude a free choice in this respect. The chords are sounded simultaneously, in this rhythm :

Measures five and six are a repetition of the first phrase, without harmony.

Then the melody and cadence harmonies of the second phrase are transferred to the relative major, measures 7 and 8. This is really simple if the relationship between *A minor* and *C major* is duly considered. The second phrase began upon the minor sub-dominant ; the fourth phrase begins on the sub-dominant of *C major.* If measures 2 and 3 were analyzed the same design can be easily transferred, as in sequence, to the third above. This phrase is to be in the key of *C.* In the latter case the same relationship is maintained, not alone in the melody, but in the harmony. Play the melody of the fourth phrase, then think of the cadence formula in the left hand, and play that.

Now join the two parts. Altogether this will constitute a short period of eight measures. Repeat it once or twice carefully.

Measures nine and ten consist of the opening phrase transposed to *C major.* This is in octaves, like the original phrase, but a third above. Play it.

Measures eleven and twelve are like three and four, but in
C major. When the notes are imagined (as they should be)
the pupil will discover that measures seven and eight and
eleven and twelve are identical. Now add the harmonization
as before, and combine the two parts—both hands.

Measures thirteen and fourteen are exactly the same as
nine and ten. Fifteen and sixteen are in *E minor.*

The melodic phrase, ten and eleven, is therefore to be played
a third higher, and according to the harmonic minor scale of *E.*
Think of the sub-dominant to *E minor,* for there the phrase
begins, and it is to be exactly like the second phrase—both
being in minor. Therefore the imperfect triad, (c.)
is to be transposed to *E minor* literally. Find the
sub-dominant as real-bass, add a third and a sixth according to
the key of *E minor* and the imperfect triad will result.* The
remainder of the harmonic cadence is now to be performed in
E minor. Play each phrase with the parts separated; then
join them.

Measure sixteen is now to be sequenced in *C major* and
A minor in order to end in the original key. (This accounts
for the four additional measures.) The melodic sequence is
here outlined:

The three tonics are a third apart, and the motive is repeated according to these scales. Think of the sequence,
then play it.

Now repeat the harmonic formula of sixteen at seventeen
and eighteen. The model is this:

---

* It is to be hoped that the pupil will not long be obliged to rely upon
this elementary transposition process. All these chords should be known
theoretically and practically (to the head and to the fingers) so that when a
formula is required in another key, as here, it can be played instantly.

Seventeen in *C major.*
Eighteen in *A minor.*

Now add a complete cadence in *A minor* and the task will end. The melody is :

The right hand has the chords here, because the bass is to be :

Omit the fifth from the dominant seventh chord above.

The entire movement of twenty measures should be repeated two or three times. The rate of speed may then be increased to (♩ = 108), and the style of performance is not to be neglected, though that is a secondary matter here.

It is presumed that this page of music will be reproduced by the student in very nearly the same manner in which the composer wrote it. The selection (of which our reproduction forms part I) is entitled thc Goblin, by H. Nürnberg, Op. 71, VI.

A considerable quantity of Haydn's and Mozart's compositions rest upon these simple fundamental harmonies or cadence formulas. See also the following, selected almost at random from a Piano Album by C. M. von Weber : "Vien' quà, dorina bella," with variations, Op. 7 ; Polonaise, Op. 21 ; *Rondo brillante*, Op. 62 ; Invitation a la Danse, Op. 65.   Any one who can execute the Op. 65 ought to be able to supply all the harmonization, with exception perhaps of the short intro- duction and a few measures of the strain in *C.*   An occasional glance at the score, to show the form of the accompaniment, should be sufficient.   The mind would thus be free to analyze the construction of the themes, and this should be ac- complished in an hour's time.

NOTE.—Some means should be devised for covering the lower staff, leaving only the upper staff exposed to view, except where the theme passes to the left hand.   This would obviate the necessity for copying the melody part.

LESSON VII.

UNRELATED TONES.

Many designs which are apparently complicated become perfectly plain when we distinguish between the related notes and those unrelated to the harmony. The suspension, the appoggiatura, and the passing note are most important to be understood here. The suspension and the appoggiatura occur on an accented part of the measure, and are unrelated to the accompanying harmony. The suspension (tied or untied) is heard previously as a harmonic tone before it becomes dissonant through retardation. Then it resolves, usually in some natural manner, to the tone above or below. The appoggiatura is similar, except that it is unprepared. Both are illustrated in the following example. The suspension is numbered 3 ; the appoggiatura, 2 ; the related note is marked 0 :

Observe that the suspension (3) was previously consonant,

or formed part of a dominant seventh chord, and then the melody note was held until the accompaniment changed to a chord of which the note marked 3 forms no part. (Compare the suspensions with the chords below.)

In example (b) the note numbered 2 evidently does not belong to the *C* minor chord, but the note following is related, having been kept back by the dissonant appoggiatura. The next is similar :

Ex. 48.

The harmonic outline is :

From this it is plainly to be seen that *G* and *B flat* are appoggiature—*i. e.*, unrelated notes falling upon the accented parts of a measure. In the next quotation *E* is technically an appoggiatura, but really an implied suspension :

Ex. 49.

E, as well as *G*, is part of the dominant seventh chord on *A*, and accordingly the effect of a suspension is produced when *E* displaces or keeps back the harmonic note, *D.* This is accompanied by the suspension of *G* below (3) resolving to *F.*

The passing note also is unrelated to the accompanying harmony, but occurs on the *unaccented* parts of a measure, thus:

The passing notes are numbered 1. Example 51 is explainable in the same way:

When the passing note or the appoggiatura is *above* the harmonic note the former is diatonic—*i. e.,* according to the key in which it occurs. But when the unrelated note is *below* the harmonic note the former is usually a minor second from its resolution. This has been the custom since the time of Bach. See Exs. 49 and 50.

The pupil may now add the harmony to the following phrase:

Appoggiatura above.

The harmony is indicated by the notes with ciphers. After discovering the chord play it in the left hand with this rhythm: | ♩ ♩ ♩ |

The appoggiatura will now be written below the principal note:

(b.)

After playing this, imagine the harmony; then join the two parts as before.

The following is similar in theory:

Ex. 53.

Continue the left hand part as indicated. This forms a perfect harmonic cadence.

The number of designs, figurations, variations and cadenzas founded upon these unrelated tones, above and below the harmonic tones, is incalculable, and, in what follows, the student's success will depend largely upon a proper understanding of the principles explained. Thus, the next figuration becomes almost simple after it is accurately analyzed:

Ex. 54.

The quarter notes plainly indicate a certain concord passing through its different close positions or re-arrangements. In each instance the accompaniment consists of two notes which (with the quarter note above) complete the chord. *B flat* and *F* are added beneath *D;* *D* and *B flat* are to be added beneath *F*, and so on. This is the harmonic outline and it ought to be apprehended at once. Play the phrase first in this form :

The figuration must be analyzed more minutely. To each beat there are four sixteenth notes in the accompaniment, and the second note of each group is to be a minor second below the first note of the group. Think of the figuration before attempting to play it. When it is sufficiently understood proceed to execute the phrase slowly, but exactly as Beethoven wrote it.

Little can be learned from seeking the solution among the master's sonatas. But after the design has been reproduced there would be no objection to such consultation. (In the original the right hand executes both parts, but they are separated here as a preliminary study.)

The same design should. be carried out with different chords, for instance :

Ex. 55.

There are two designs to be understood : one harmonic, the other melodic. The former is simple :

The melodic figures below will (until the pupil has become expert) require close attention.

A design with diatonic and chromatic passing notes will now be undertaken. Each sequence figure is a third below

its antecedent. From the first to the second note of every
triplet figure is either a normal or an imperfect fourth ; but
the second to the third note is invariably a minor second. The
third note, like the first, is always diatonic :

Not until the design is well understood should its execution
be attempted. Then the movement must be sufficiently slow
to preclude the possibility of error. Continue downward until
a natural cadence is effected, thus :

Transpose the entire passage, increasing the movement
gradually. After the ending, Ex. (b) the section may be repeated an octave lower.

Those who understand harmonization may add a chord
accompaniment in the left hand. Perhaps this form would
be best :

Continue the following design two or three octaves :

All the lower passing tones (1) are to be a minor second from the harmonic or principal tones.

Play similar figures descending :

The passing tones here are all diatonic.   Harmonize both designs.   If there were no other parts it would be well to play these cadenza passages with both hands alternately.   Increase the speed to allegro, and transpose.

LESSON VIII.

UNRELATED TONES CONTINUED.

GRUPPETTI.

Appoggiature and passing notes above and below lead naturally to the gruppetto, or turn, usually represented by the symbol (a):

Ex. 59.

The point to observe is, that the principal tone, *C*, is embellished with passing tones next above and below, and that the former does not lose its harmonic nor its melodic identity. The turn may begin at once on the tone above, and even then the harmonic tone will be heard twice:

The student may now embellish the following outlines above, according to Ex. 59, (c) and (d):

Ex. 60.

(48)

For some of the transpositions the student should add the remaining notes of the chord beneath each group above ; *C* and *E flat* (in the left hand) beneath *A flat; E flat* and *A flat* beneath *C*, and so on. After completing one octave in this manner there will be nothing new to learn, however high or low the design may be carried.

The inverted gruppetto is next in order. Here the notes of the direct gruppetto are reversed :

Ex. 61.

Continue in the manner indicated ; also transpose to *F sharp, F, E, E flat*, and *D*. At least one example should be written by the student that the eye may become accustomed to their appearance when fully notated.

The following figuration has been used in various ways by different composers :

Ex. 62.

Down a second, up a third, and down a second, describes the figure in a general way. But it must be understood that from the first to the second tone of each group is invariably a minor second. All the other tones are to be diatonic. The interval of a third is sometimes minor and at other times diminished—never major. In executing the design for the right hand follow the harmonic outlines of the chord in the left hand :

This figuration should be played upon the sub-dominant and upon the dominant in regular succession, ending upon the tonic.   Make a period in this style.

Also the following is recommended for practice :

Ex. 63.

(Continue two or three octaves.)   Transpose and increase the movement gradually.

Finally, the motive, 62, is to be performed in scale sequence.   The figures are to be constructed in the same manner as described :

Ex. 64.

A similar figuration is continued in an ascending movement in Beethoven's Op. 2, III.   See the cadenza to the first allegro.   After observing the form of the cadenza, close the music pages and perform it as written.

These examples of unrelated notes, together with the direct and inverted anschlag,

Ex. 65.

form the basis of nearly all embellishments, variations, cadenzas, etc.   By understanding the theory and application of

---

*See the *Rondo brillante* in *E flat* by von Weber.

these unrelated notes one is enabled to seize at once upon melodic outlines, and thus penetrate the composer's design. The outlines, to which attention has so frequently been directed, are all-important in reproducing a passage of music, because, when these are understood, it is not a difficult task to add the detail. Thus the following section of twenty-eight notes can be played readily from the first four notes, which constitute the model. Of course, this must be analyzed:

BEETHOVEN.

Ex. 66.

The chord below shows the harmonic outline; the passing notes a minor second below each interval of the *D minor* triad form the detail. There are seven of these descending groups, but it is unnecessary to read more than one. Consequently the entire passage can be mastered in one-seventh of the time usually devoted to "memorizing" such figurations. And furthermore, when a design is re-created according to this method, the music becomes an individual possession—we feel that, to a certain extent, it is ours—and there is little probability that it will be soon forgotten. But when the actual notes are merely memorized, they are liable to escape us at the most critical time, because the act of memorizing is irrational—it leaves no mental impress—and the mind is still unconscious of the composer's design and of the basic theory of music structure.

The passing note figures are resumed:

PAGANINI.

Ex. 67.

L. H.

Begin by analyzing the melodic figures. The first of the two sixteenth notes is always a minor second below the fol-

lowing related note.   Otherwise the notes above merely form
the *B flat* chord.   Continue the theme mentally before
playing it.

The left hand merely supplies the harmony below, all in
close position, as previously explained.

Combine the two parts and continue in sequence form two
or three octaves below.

In ascending with this figuration it will be necessary to
disperse the upper part (a), or repeat the last melody note of
each group (b):

It would be well to play these in several keys, impromptu.
Similar figurations will be encountered in modern music, and
the student should be familiar with their structure.

Ex. 69 is not so simple, but it is musical and consistent :

This is a somewhat ornate elaboration of the common *D*
chord, as shown by the triad in parenthesis, below.   Observe
especially that the group begins and ends with a note belong-
ing to the harmony ; and that the void between *A* and *D* is
filled by two passing notes.   But an important tonal consider-
ation enters here: the intervals between the different positions of the common chord are disproportionate.   From the
fifth to the upper root-note is a normal fourth ; from the third
to the fifth is a small third ; from root to third is a large
third.   Accordingly, in order to maintain the characteristic
feature of the design, it will be necessary to employ three
kinds of passing notes : diatonic, chromatic and mixed.   Only
in this way can we arrange to have the first and last notes of

each group form parts of the *D* chord. Hence the ciphers
and figures, indicating related and unrelated notes. Every
note of the second and third groups should be seen mentally
before attempting to execute them. The first and fourth
notes of each group are first to be determined upon, thus:

Then fill in the two passing notes, diatonically or chromatically, as the intervals of the chord may require. The
next example shows the harmonic and the passing notes
separately:

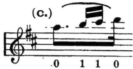

Continue downward several octaves. Play slow at first,
avoiding mistakes of all kinds.

An accompaniment may be added when the movement is
quickened. Various forms are available for the left hand part.
Transpose to *E, F, F sharp*, and *G*. The fact is to be understood that in continuing such motives as 67 and 69, the performer must be guided by the intervals of the chord to be
elaborated, not by the strict order of melodic sequence. For
instance, if we repeat literally the figure of Ex. 69 (a), we
would produce a sequence (b), but not such a design as was
intended (a). Both methods are here illustrated:

A glance at the score would tell whether the composer
intended a harmonic figuration design, as at (a), or a simple
melodic sequence, as at (b).

LESSON IX.

PASSING NOTE FIGURES.

The last figuration (69 and 70 a) is to be applied to other chords, and it is advisable to employ both hands alternately. Since this figure passes through the various intervals of a given chord the harmonic effect is sufficiently complete without other accompaniment. An outline is here presented, and this is to be completed by the student :

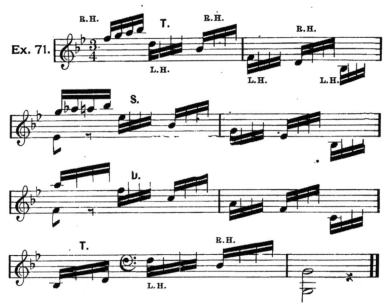

Ex. 71.

Repeat this period until it can be performed accurately, and in moderate tempo, without notes. Then transpose to B, C, C sharp, D, E flat, E, and F.

What was said about following the chord outlines in Ex. 69 (a) applies to the next design :

Ex. 72.

The left hand has a triplet figure with a passing note in the middle. The right hand has a similar figure a fifth above. At 3 the left hand begins a major third above its first figure; but at 4 the right hand is not to begin a fifth above *G sharp*, because the harmonic indication is evidently this dominant chord :

The cadenza is built upon this plain harmony slightly embellished, as indicated at (a). All this should be discovered at once, and then the two hands are to be employed in executing the design. Understood in this sense, the cadenza is actually simple. Play it, moderato, to the altissimo compass; then descend in similar manner. Repeat, allegro, and transpose.

A different scheme is now presented :

Ex. 73.

Here there are two motives, or rather a subject above and counter-subject below, to be continued in diatonic sequence. The task is not a simple one, and unless it be carefully considered the student will certainly fail. Begin each group, ♩♩♩♩, a diatonic fourth above the previous ♩ of the melody, and continue this for six measures. The quarter notes on the first of each measure descend scalewise. This is part of the design, and it must be ever present to the mind while the sequence is in progress.

The bass part forms a regular sequence after the first note, which is substituted for *E.* Hence, in the second measure, the lower group of  will begin a fifth, not a third, below the ♩ on the first beat. Now perform the left hand part separately and repeat.

The upper cadence is this :

The bass may be fundamental—tonic, sub-dominant and dominant in the seventh measure—which is characteristic of the Haendel epoch.

In combining the two parts proceed with the utmost deliberation, keeping before the mind's eye both motives. The dissonances are rather harsh, but they are of brief duration and effective. Continue to practice 73 until it can be played moderately fast in any key and without a mistake.

PASSING NOTES AND APPOGGIATURE.

A theme composed principally of unrelated notes here follows :

B. WOLFF, op. 158, III.

The second measure is similar to the first; the fourth measure is very nearly like the third. Observe that at 1 the harmony passes from tonic to dominant; at 2 this order is reversed. Then there is a modulation to the relative minor, and back to the major tonic of *A*. For purposes of analysis all the melodic notes are marked : 1, passing note; 2, appoggiatura ; 3, suspension ; 0, harmonic.

Transpose the theme to *A flat* and add the harmony. **Same in *G*.**

LESSON X.

CHROMATIC SEQUENCE.   INTERCHANGEABLE PARTS.

To one who is familiar with all major and minor keys and with modulation, there is nothing strange in the appearance of chromatic passages and transitions. Theoretically, the key of *F* is merely a chromatic step below the key of *F sharp;* their structure is identical and their tonal relations are relatively the same. But one must have had considerable experience to be able to tell at a glance whether chromatic notes are used in a transitional or in a passive capacity.

A chromatic motive is quoted :

This is a strict chromatic sequence. When the motive is analyzed continue it two octaves. The outline is this :

Repeat allegro.

The next is similar, though it employs both hands :

---

* The marks of abbreviation, ▬ ▬, indicate similar, but not identical, groups in continuation of the model.

(58)

First observe the chromatic steps, because these continue chromatically in both parts. The interval from the second note of the left hand to the first note of the right hand is either an augmented second or a minor third. (On all keyed instruments these are identical.) This interval is maintained throughout. Continue up and down two or three octaves, moderately. Then repeat allegro.

A more complicated design follows :

A musician would play this very readily by considering the design as a series of normal fourths descending chromatically thus :

It is to be observed that both parts descend by half-steps, not only here, but in the original form.

It might be well at first to execute the cadenza in this manner, with both hands; then with one hand alone, as in Ex. 77 (a).

When the preceding is mastered the left hand part is to be added immediately below, in this rhythm : | ♫ ♩ ♫ ♩ |. Consider each normal fourth above as root and fifth of a major chord. The fourths alone are ambiguous and require the characteristic tone to complete the effect. The student is to dis-

cover this characteristic tone which accompanies each couplet
of sixteenth notes above. The left hand part descends chromatically. Combine the two parts and continue downward at
least one octave. Then, when the progressions have returned
to *D*, endeavor to effect a satisfactory close by means of an
authentic cadence and the same rhythm.

Since the last cadenza passes through all the major chords
it is not essential that the example should be transposed.

INTERCHANGEABLE PARTS.

The following figuration is to be analyzed and then played
through several measures :

The better way is to conceive each group (ascending third
and ascending sixth) as beginning a diatonic tone below the
preceding, thus :

This serves to reveal the melodic delineation, which is
always important. The process last described will impress
upon the mind Beethoven's design more firmly (and more
quickly) than would the actual melodic analysis : up a third,
down a fifth, and up a sixth. This is too primitive for the
situation, and besides it does not condense or epitomize the
figuration as does the Ex. (b). According to this the entire
scheme is plainly revealed. Play the section in this manner,
slowly.

Also ,the harmonic form may be considered, showing the
dominant relation :

This does not add to, nor interfere with, the melodic outline in quarter notes, already indicated. Continue the harmonic sequence (c) to a cadence on *A flat*.

A new feature now appears. The left hand part as Beethoven wrote it consists of what the author, in his new system of Synthetic Counterpoint, calls interchangeable, or reciprocal counterpoint. This the student may invent according to a simple principle. Every two notes above, which belong to a certain chord, are to be read backward (like retrograde canon) and played by the left hand an octave lower as contrapuntal accompaniment.

Thus *C* and *E* would be accompanied by *E* and *C*, as here:

Ex. 79.

In this way the entire passage can be played impromptu from the theme alone, if one is accustomed to rapid thinking. When the upper part is accomplished, the student should add the interchangeable counterpoint in the left hand and thus continue, slow at first.

One form of cadence is given in case it may be needed:

Ex. 80.

The two last sixteenth notes are not to be accompanied reciprocally.

The following is a similar design, to be continued at greater length:

The student is to fill in these outlines as indicated. Then add the interchangeable part below. This also is to be played separately—unless the performer is very confident that the concert needs no rehearsing.

The figure of Ex. 81 is to be reversed and continued in an ascending movement. Repeat this, and then, from the upper motive, construct the consonant counterpoint for the left hand according to the interchangeable principle. The design is given:

Combine the parts for both hands, and follow the ascending design for an octave or more.

Beethoven employed a variety of these figurations in his piano sonatas, and nearly all are accompanied reciprocally. See Op. 26, finale ; and Op. 54, the rondo.

Transpose 82 into several other keys.

The next problem is more difficult of solution :

---

* In the original score these parts were inverted (the theme alternately below and above), but for simplicity's sake this plan has been altered.

The first phrase is in *F minor*. This is repeated in *E flat major*. The melody and harmony of the second phrase have the same relationship to *E flat* that melody and harmony of the first phrase have to *F minor*. This tonal principle is infallible; whereas if the student undertakes to transpose the first phrase literally a major second lower the result will be a failure. The author suggests that the left hand part (having the theme) be played alone in the two keys, as outlined.

Then perform the figurated accompaniment slow, observing its relationship to the theme below. The second phrase is thematically similar.

After the two parts are well understood, they are of course to be performed simultaneously.

The continuation of 83 (a) is this:

The same figuration accompanies this return of the motive to *A flat*. That part which is bracketed is an addenda, and the student may invent an accompaniment to this in the same rhythm, ♩♪♪♪ ♩♪♪♪ .

When these two parts are mastered and joined together, play the entire eight measures (Exs. 83 a and b) continuously.

Transpose the period into other keys, beginning upon the dominant seventh of the relative minor.

LESSON XI.

HARMONIC AND MELODIC SEQUENCES MODULATING.

In the next example there is a melodic sequence above and a harmonic sequence below. They are rather neutral in character, neither wholly strict nor wholly free. The entire period is to be constructed from the model contained in the first measure. It is a scheme which has been employed by various composers:

Ex. 84. (a.)

Analyze the melody separately. Observe the two figures, and that from *E minor* the music modulates to the natural key a third below. Each measure begins upon the third of each new key. Include the necessary chromatic notes in passing to *A minor* and to *F major*. Also be particular to play the two first notes of each group in strict sequence—*i. e.*, a minor second (as *G* to *F sharp*), and a major second, *G* to *F natural.* See the first combination figure of eight notes. Play the right hand part slow and repeat.

The sequence below is strict : a normal fifth, quarter rest, and minor sixth. The lower tone of the sixth is the leading note to the new key, and therefore resolves up a minor second in every instance. The modulations proceed by the third relation downward: *E, C, A, F.* The second chord in every measure is to be the dominant (with third as real bass) to the following key. All this must be understood if success is to be attained. (If in doubt as to the result, re-read this paragraph and observe the example to which it refers.) Continue this scheme until it ends in *F* at the end of the first section.

The next step consists in joining the two parts, slowly at first, then a little faster.

The second section begins on the *A minor* chord, measure 5, and ends in *C* at 8:

The regular order of sequence must be discontinued at 7 else it will run into *B flat*, which is not here desirable. The cadence in *C* may be made in various ways, but this is left to the ingenuity of the student. Complete the period and repeat until it is mastered. Then add the harmonization as indicated. A complete cadence should occur at the end.

After combining the two parts in the last section, repeat the entire period of eight measures from the beginning, Ex. 84 (a). Endeavor to do this without hesitating, even though the movement be quite slow. No worse mistake can be committed than that of stumbling or stammering, and thus interrupting the movement of the music.

Finally, transpose to at least four other keys. (Six or eight would be better.)

The last design is an important one, and the author recommends that it be thoroughly mastered. As an aid to the inexperienced two solutions of the final cadence are presented:

In the last ending *A flat* assists somewhat in diverting the sequence back to *C major.*

Ex. 86 is a motive intended to be carried to a conclusion according to the same principles :

The melodic sequence of this, whether in major or minor, is to be strict; that is to say, each scale figure begins upon a dominant and ascends to the following tonic, two major seconds and one minor second.   Hence, when the modulation is to a related minor key, the ascending form of the melodic minor scale is to be used.   In this scale, 5, 6, 7, 8 are identical in both modes, thus :

We proceed with the design.   The next scale figure begins a diatonic tone above *G* and passes to its upper tonic.   Imagine this.

The question arises here, shall this be *D major or D minor?*   The answer is contained in this brief statement. The related keys to a major tonic are—tonic, sub-dominant, dominant, and the relative minors of these.   In minor they are—tonic, sub-dominant, and dominant (all minor) and their relative majors.   If the student is unskilled in modulation he or she may consult this chart of the related keys (here represented by the chords) in *C:*

These triads merely represent the related keys; but, in order to establish a new key, we must introduce into the melody or the harmony some tone foreign to the old key and characteristic of the new.

Having modulated to *D minor* in the second measure, include the major second below on the last beat (corresponding to *B flat* in the first measure), as this tone serves to prepare the ear for the following modulation.

The sequence at 3 is to be constructed mentally in the same manner; and do not forget that each succeeding tone must be a natural tone of the original scale—*C* in this instance. Therefore do not attempt to modulate to *E flat*, nor to *F sharp*. Ex. 88 will tell whether *E* is to be major or minor.

When the motive has passed in sequence form through *C*, *D minor*, *E minor*, *F*, *G*, and *A minor*, it should then return in some natural way to *C major* on the eighth measure. Repeat the melody part.

The accompaniment is to be conceived (before it is played) in this manner: To what key do the three first notes lead? (Answer.) Now think of the dominant seventh to that key. When the leading note, which is the third of the dominant seventh chord, appears prominently in an upper part, the third would better be omitted from the accompanying discord. Likewise the fifth is omitted below when that note appears prominently above. This usually prevents parallel octaves and is certainly clearer, thus:

BEETHOVEN.

Ex. 89.

The figures show that the interval wanting in the lower chord is supplied by the theme. Particularly observe both measures.

We now return to the harmonization of Ex. 86. The rhythm is to be | ♩. ♩ ⸯ | in each measure as far as the final cadence. The accompaniment is merely dominant seventh and tonic repeated by means of transposition in six related keys. Play the left hand part alone two or three times, after it has been evolved mentally.

The conclusion may be effected in this way:

The descending scale figures here are contrary inversions of the original motive, and therefore perfectly relevant.

Complete the perfect cadence first. Since the melody sounds the third and fifth of the dominant seventh chord the accompaniment may be played as at (a) or as at (b):

Now play the entire period uninterruptedly, and repeat two or three times.

In transposing the period play the theme and the accompaniment separately at first.

The following is to be continued in sequence six measures:

The motive (first used by Mozart in a piano sonata) is easily analyzed. Every ascending broken chord is in its first position. Also the rhythmic arrangement is the same in measures 2, 3, and 4. Name the notes of the three sequences before sounding them. Then no difficulty will be experienced.

The harmonic progressions form a series of third relations. This has been explained. But surely no composer would arrange the chord in these parallels :

The connecting notes (keys) are to be played by the same fingers. *F* and *A* therefore are retained in going from 1 to 2. All that remains, is to move the thumb from the *C* to the *D* key. Use this rhythm :

Complete the four measures as explained. The harmonies below must accord with the theme above. In fact, the latter indicates the chords of the accompaniment.

The fifth measure should appear like this :

(See the Ex. from Beethoven, 89 ; also 91.)

Soon as both parts are well understood, combine them and play the short period as outlined. Always repeat, and increase the movement after each repetition.

Transpose to *E*, *E flat*, *D*, and *D flat*.

For the remaining transpositions advanced students may improve the harmony by means of chromatic passing notes between the whole steps.   *C sharp*, for instance, will come between *C* and *D;* and *D flat* between *D* and *C* in descending.

An outline is given :

Ex. 93.

Perhaps this should be rehearsed separately before combining it with the theme.

LESSON XII.

CHORD SEQUENCES; FREE AND STRICT.

In harmonic sequence there are two features to be particularly observed.

1. The species of chord or chords employed in the model.
2. The position in which the chords occur.

A very simple design is the following, if these two points are duly considered:

Ex. 94.

The first chord is rather vacuous, and therefore the characteristic tone (wanting above) is to be included below as real-bass. This naturally resolves up a minor second to the following tonic. Every other chord is uninverted (root in the bass) with its third above. Also observe that the movements of the parts are contrary and oblique. There is nothing more to the design as a model for the ensuing diatonic sequence. But if we analyze all the voice-parts it will be a difficult matter to construct the sequence as intended—that is, impromptu and without hesitating. For a complete analysis four staffs would be required, thus:

(b.)

To remember all these voice progressions and apply them
readily in the sequence would be a task which the author
could not conscientiously impose upon the student.   But if
the positions of the chords are carefully noted, they can be
continued downward in free sequence without experiencing
any real difficulty.   The alternate connecting notes, first in
the tenor and then in the contralto, aid considerably in executing the passage.   Of course, the melodic formula must not
be allowed to escape the attention, even for a moment ; but
that is simple.   Continue to the cadence on *C,* an octave below
the beginning.

It is a curious fact that this harmonic sequence should
pass twice through what may be termed a diatonic cycle.   By
means of the dominant relation it progresses through every
tone in the key and returns naturally to the tonic.   This appears more plainly when the bass is fundamental :

Ex. 95. (a.)

Diatonic Cycle.   *Ditto.*

It would be beneficial to play the full harmony above from
this fundamental part.   In dominant progressions (up a fourth
or down a fifth) there is always one connecting note, and this
is to remain as such.   Since none of the basses here are inverted, the chords above are not to appear alternately in half-
open position (first chord, Ex. 94, a), but in this form :

Include also the other two close positions, same bass. Observe the order in which the three species of triad occur: How many major chords in succession? How many minor? And where does the imperfect triad appear?

Transpose to *B flat, A flat,* and *G.*

Ex. 94 should be transferred to minor, using the mixed form of scale, thus:

Ex. 96.

The second chord in every measure is in its first inversion, as it was in Ex. 94. The upper part should be varied, as here:

Transpose to various other minor keys.

A series of harmonic sequences here follow:

Ex. 97.

These diatonic sequences in the old classic style are naturally free. Take particular notice of the position of the two first chords, and the alternate connecting notes. It ought to be an easy task to continue in this style. The bass is still more simple. Play each part once or twice separately. They may then be combined and continued to a cadence on *D,* an octave below the beginning.

Transpose to *E flat, E, F, F sharp, G,* and *A flat.*

The next design is not so simple:

Ex. 98.

The chords above appear in only two positions, though there are two passing discords in every measure. Compose the upper parts in a sequence, mentally, until the scheme is well understood. Then play the four parts as indicated.

The next is similar:

Ex. 99.

The actual model to be reproduced is that within the bracket. Hence the sequence begins at measure three. The design involves a series of discords, mostly secondary; yet every dissonant interval is resolved to a consonant. This is an important principle and will be illustrated here: The first dissonance occurs when the bass sings *D*, and this disappears when the *D* is succeeded by *C.* Here the middle upper voice-part sings *A flat*, which dissonates with the suspended *G* below. Then *G* is followed by *F*, which is consonant to *A flat.*

Write two or three measures that the discords and their consonant resolutions may be traced. It is to be observed that 2 resolves to 3, 7 to 6, and 9 to 10. This formula is a direct aid to sight reading, as well as to this theory for re-creating a given passage.

---

* In the transpositions omit the ties. On a piano this will give the pupil a better impression as to the actual effect of the discords individually.

LESSON XIII.

CHORD INVERSION (DISPERSED HARMONY).

MOTIVE INVERSION.

Dispersed harmony has become the rule rather than the exception in modern piano music, and the student should be familiar with the theory and practice of chord inversion. The former is quite simple: Suppose a concord to be in its first close position (a); by inverting the middle note an octave higher (b), or an octave lower (c), an open position will result, thus:

Ex. 100.   (a.)   (b.)   (c.)

The chord does not lose its identity on account of these open positions (b) and (c); the root is still *B flat*, as shown at (a).

The student may now play the following triads in open positions by inverting *the middle note an octave higher* in every instance:

Ex. 101.

Of course, this will alter the upper melody notes, but that need not be considered here since the exercise is essentially harmonic.

Play the same example, two octaves lower, with the left hand.

The following is to be in dispersed harmony above, with the roots below :

Ex. 102.

These melodic notes are to remain uppermost.   Therefore the remaining intervals are to be played below, as :   ·

In the majority of instances there would be a difference between these two illustrations, but that need not detain us here.   The author merely suggests that these open positions be practiced moderately and distinctly, but mezzo-piano.   The hand should be in an extended position with the fingers as nearly as possible over the required keys before the latter are pressed down.   Since every pianist must be ambidextrous, it will be necessary to practice open positions as much with the left hand as with the right hand.   Transpose Ex. 102 into several major and minor keys.

The dominant seventh chord is next in order.   A simple method consists in writing the re-arrangements in close position as a guide, thus :

Re-arrangements. *

Ex. 103.

---

* In his harmony system the author does not apply the word **inversion** to these close positions.   Technically the chord is not inverted unless the real-bass has some other note than the root.

In every position here the note next to the lowest† is the one to be inverted an octave higher. Practice this in dispersed harmony with each hand separately. Then transpose through all the keys.

After a few examples like 103 have been written as guides, dispense with the notes altogether.

The manner in which these open and half-open positions are used may be seen here:

Slumber Song.

The works of modern composers contain many instances of dispersed harmonies, some of which are much more extended. For instance:

Flirtation.

FROM RUSSIAN VILLAGE SUITE.

MOTIVE INVERSION.

Reference is here made to the inversion of a principal theme, either above or below, especially where the theme is accompanied with a counter-subject or other characteristic counterpoint. A simple example is quoted:

Ex. 106.

The motive (S.) for the left hand is inverted two octaves above for the right hand, meanwhile the counter-subject (C. S.) appears first above and then below.

The principles of inversion can not all be understood except by those who have mastered counterpoint ; but in its common application no difficulty should be experienced. It is illustrated in the resolution of these upper and lower leading notes :

Ex. 107.

The resolutions at (a) and at (b) are identical; the first is to tonic and third, the second is to third and tonic. In the inversion of S. and C. S. this principle is to be applied.

The student may now reverse the order of S. and C. S. in the following phrase :

Ex. 108.

After observing the design critically, invert the S. an octave higher and the C. S. an octave lower.

Then continue in this manner :

The following is similar:

Beginning on the fifth measure the subject is to be inverted two octaves lower, the counter-subject one octave higher. Each part is repeated literally in a different compass.

The same design is to be transposed a fifth lower and inverted. This will bring the cadence upon *E flat*.

The theme from Haendel is inverted strictly, but the accompaniment is slightly altered when it is transposed to the right hand:

Each part is to be examined away from the instrument until it can be played without notes. (This can be done as soon as the design is analyzed). Then, at 5, the theme is repeated an octave lower, while the modified accompaniment is to be played an octave higher.

The next quotation is not so simple:

The S. and C. S. pass through various keys, but the parts are not here interchangeable. Fortunately the two parts are antiphonal. After what was quoted there are no more chromatic signs required.

End in *B flat* with the motive figure.

Of course, the parts are to be rehearsed separately. Transpose, and then invert the entire section.

Other examples may, and perhaps should, be selected.

In the finale to Beethoven's Op. 27, II, the second subject appears twice in an inverted form. In all such instances the inversion is to be reproduced without notes (or from the model) as illustrated in this lesson.

LESSON XIV.

FREE SEQUENCE STRUCTURE IN TWO PARTS—ATTEMPT TO REPRODUCE A CRAMER ETUDE.

From a few motive figures the student will now attempt to build a music structure more or less complete. Analyze every figure as previously directed :

There is a note lacking in the first group, and this must be imagined in order to understand that the sequence is really regular. Continue each figure two or three octaves. This one evidently ascends.

Add a part for the left hand six notes below Ex. (a), and play this separately, slow at first.

Combine the two parts (they are in parallel sixths) and continue upward. No cadences are to be included at present.

The next figure is this :

Continue downward two octaves.

The left hand part embraces two figures :

Observe particularly the second group and the interval preceding. Then continue downward with the left hand.

It will not be a difficult task to combine the two parts (**b** and c) if they have been analyzed separately.

Figure (d) is similar to (b):

This can be played readily.

The left hand part is but little varied. It is in sixths. Each figure begins a second above the last note of the previous figure. (This is important to know.)

There is a measure not in sequence form, but otherwise quite simple. It is a melodic motive in the left hand part, thus:

In order to maintain the rhythm of sixteenth notes, the *C* next above is included between (or after) every melodic note below. The main feature to be impressed upon the mind is the chromatic progression from *E* to *A*.

A new figure is now introduced:

The three notes in parenthesis are preparatory and do not appear in the sequence. The trill figures continue to descend in the manner indicated.

The left hand has this consonant counterpoint:

Each group begins a tone lower. Continue two measures separately, then combine (f) and (g).

The following is still different and must be carefully observed:

The last group is to be more especially noted. Observe the parts separately, and then conjointly.

The next measure is here outlined:

The figuration is a series of quasi trill groups like (h). The left hand part below forms the following intervals which can easily be continued in sequence: A minor third, an octave and two sixths. (See last group, Ex. h.) This is so even here:

A design in suspension now appears. This represents two voices, though it is executed by the right hand, thus:

Continue these outlines.

The figuration is easily added, being similar to (j):

(l.)

The upper note in every other figure is a suspension (and the note below is to be a minor second in the sequence, as it is in the model). Therefore the intervals are: 7 to 6, 7 to 6. A different design appears in the accompanying part:

(m.)

This should be played separately before it is joined to the design in suspension (k) and (l).

The four last measures may be thus outlined :

(n.) (Continue) all R.H.

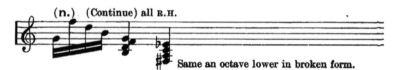

Same an octave lower in broken form.

The rhythm of sixteenths continues; also here :

(o.)

If the pupil will repeat all the figures from Ex. 113 (a), and particularly observe the designs, or mode of construction, the famous Etude in *C* by J. B. Cramer will have been mastered. By referring to the printed copy (No. 1 in Hatch edition) the formal arrangement and the few remaining details may be seen and easily joined together.

There are three phrases (or rhythms) in the last half of the etude containing three measures each. These begin upon 10, 13, and 16. The last phrase has four measures. In comprehending the entire study it is important to know these peculiarities of structure.*

According to this mode of procedure the etude ought to be learned in less than two hours' time, instead of consuming a week's time, as it usually does. Etudes 2 and 10 are similar.

---

* In another work the author has indicated the particular manner in which these uneven rhythms should be performed.

LESSON XV.

CANONIC IMITATIONS.

To the student of imitation and fugue, all music in canonic style* is half mastered as soon as its structure is observed.

Canon signifies law, or rule; and the consequent voice merely sings the same theme (approximately) as that of the antecedent, in whatever interval may be indicated by the composer. The most primitive illustration consists of a scale theme answered in the unison, identically, after the lapse of one measure :

Ex. 114.

Beginning at the second measure the left hand plays the same notes as those of the right hand. Therefore the consequent ends on the tonic at 7, as the antecedent did at 6.

After a brief examination of the design the two parts are to be played at sight.

Selections are here made from the 200 Short Canons by Konrad Kunz.† While these serve many useful purposes, especially in sight-reading, they are treated somewhat differently here. The motive only of No. 5 is quoted :

Ex. 115.

(a.)   (b.)

---

* This includes nearly all of the music of the 17th Century, considerable of the 18th, and many high-class works from modern composers.

† The composer is not responsible for those five pages of injudicious, useless " questions and answers " in the beginning.

No other melodic material is used for this canon of eight measures. Therefore it seems unnecessary to write or to read the right hand part ; it should be re-created. After the lapse of one measure the consequent begins an octave higher and repeats this motive. When it is sufficiently analyzed in its melodic and rhythmic aspects, play it as written, but without notes.

Now add the consequent in this manner : On the second measure the right hand begins an octave higher and plays the same motive. When the right hand has played the first four notes the left hand has concluded the motive. And while the left hand begins the second half of the phrase (b), the right hand begins again as at (a). Then the right hand will play (a) while the left hand is playing (b). There is nothing more to this canon in the octave, except to make a cadence on *A minor* in the eighth measure.

Another method which the author has devised consists in singing the consequent part while the motive is repeated on the piano or organ as an accompaniment. In this case the voice enters as before on the second measure, sings the motive, and repeats.

After the vocal test it would be easy to play the canon in similar manner. Transpose to *G minor* and *F minor*, and play from the motive only.

The antecedent of another canon is quoted :

After Ex. 116. — No. 21, Kunz Canons.

Analyze this thoroughly ; then play it rather slowly with the right hand, and afterward an octave lower with the left hand ; and without consulting the notes.

Before attempting the canon (it is not a canon until the antecedent and consequent are combined), compose it mentally until the structure is well understood. The rests below in Ex. 116 show exactly where the left hand part enters. The two notes marked * * are always unaccompanied, whether above or below. The bracket indicates the last half of the motive. The first half always enters simultaneously (in another voice) with the second half. Repeat as indicated.

In the cadence the response is curtailed, thus:

Repeat without interrupting the movement.

A more extended theme follows:

The same directions apply here. The theme is to be analyzed and then played with the right hand until the design becomes quite familiar.

The consequent enters on the third measure—on what interval? and imitates the theme strictly.

In repeating from measure eight, the lower part is not to be interrupted but continue with its theme. At the final cadence the consequent is curtailed and ends thus:

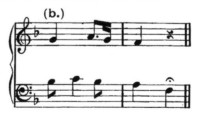

Begin adagio and increase the movement to moderato.

It will suffice to quote the motive of the next canon, especially as it is simple :

Ex. 118.

No. 118.

(a.   (b.)

Left hand part an octave lower.

The semi-phrases (a and b) show the manner in which antecedent and consequent are combined.

In taking leave of this very useful volume of little canons, the author suggests that several others be reproduced in the manner here indicated. Even when they are read as written, the task is greatly simplified if one knows the method by which canons are constructed. Several of the Kunz canons are written with free imitations, in various intervals. For instance: 16, 31, 41, 52, 95, 120, 132, 134, 142. These should be omitted until the canons in the octave have been well rehearsed.

The next motive is to be continued downward to a cadence. The first step is to become familiar with the right hand part in sequence form :

Dom. Scarlatti.

(a.)

Ex. 119.

This is a species of what the author calls dialogue imitation. Two solutions are practicable. The imitation in the seventh below (free) interferes slightly with the holding note of the right hand. (This would be better adapted to string instruments.) Therefore begin the left hand part, after a half measure rest, a tenth below the first note of the motive. Both parts descend by regular diatonic degrees; but it is perhaps easier to execute the canonic imitations by following this formula : The beginning of each group in the left hand is a sixth below the last half note of the right hand. The two parts always come together on a consonant interval (a sixth and a thirteenth alternately). By retaining the positions of the hands and fingers during each motive figure, it will be easy to move the hands separately down to the next diatonic note, or key.

A cadence can be effected after this group in the right hand :

In joining the two parts it may be necessary to proceed at a very slow pace.   Even an adagio movement is preferable to the stuttering and stammering which mars the practice of too many pupils.

Transpose 119 to *C, D flat,* and *D.*

LESSON XVI.

CANONIC IMITATIONS CONCLUDED.

A motive from J. S. Bach is selected, and the student is to build a short piece from this, but without attempting to strictly follow in that master's footsteps :

Ex. 120.

At first continue this in sequence with the right hand, either up or down. Of course, the design is to be carefully noted.

Play a similar sequence with the left hand separately.

We will now attempt the dialogue imitation—a species of canon. Play the motive again and immediately after the third beat, measure one, play an imitation with the left hand, a fourth below. (This is the order which Bach employed so frequently—*i. e.*, tonic answered by dominant, and vice versa.) The left hand part will end on *A* in the second measure, and the right hand will begin again on *D*, immediately after the half note below.

By way of reference a brief indication is given :

Continue slowly in this style eight measures. Then **the**
motive is to be reversed—a device which Bach frequently
employed :

Motive reversed.

The consequent here imitates the antecedent a fifth **below.**
Maintain this interval between the parts until a cadence **is**
effected in the sixteenth measure.

When this has been sufficiently rehearsed, the student
should play at sight the first of Bach's two-part Inventions.
The fact will then appear that this invention (usually considered dry as well as difficult by young players) is very **well**
understood and interesting withal.

The inventions IV, VI, VIII and XIII are especially
recommended as supplements to this lesson, and it is to be
regretted that these fine thematic and rhythmic studies are not
used more generally in place of those unmusical exercises **and**
etudes which tend to corrupt rather than to elevate the
standard of taste. Even from a merely technical standpoint
the inventions are superior. Furthermore, their structure is
highly artistic, they cultivate the rhythmic sense, and simplify
the execution of all future problems.

Another illustration of dialogue imitation is quoted :

It is the figure beneath the bracket that is imitated in the
fifth below. Play each part separately, at least four measures.

The more advanced student should endeavor to continue such designs to a logical, if not a purely artistic, conclusion. It is only in this manner that one may become expert and thus grow into a certain fellowship with the composer, which will unlock the note-bound doors of every musical seance.

A continuous theme is now quoted:

REINECKE, op. 47, II.

Ex. 122.

The similarity between certain phrases is to be noted, and this, together with the natural charm of the melody, will enable one to speedily master the thematic material. Until this is accomplished the canon is not to be attempted.

The next step consists in playing the theme with the left hand an octave lower, note for note. Since there is only one point at which the consequent can conveniently enter, the author will not indicate this, but leave the discovery to the student. When the parts have been several times rehearsed separately they may be joined in canonic style, quite slowly at first. The feat is not a simple one, but proper preparation and keen attention to the design will result successfully.

These preliminary studies will materially lessen the difficulties usually encountered in such work as the canon in Grieg's Op. 38 (a fine specimen of harmonized canon), and that beautiful illustration of imitation in Schumann's "Kreisleriana," No. III.

LESSON XVII.

PERIOD CONSTRUCTION—FORM.

An important aid in mastering the composer's transcript is furnished by a knowledge of the various methods employed in building a music structure by periods.

The most important principle, sequence in some of its phases, is nearly always present. This has been illustrated quite fully. Therefore we will pass on.

LYRIC MUSIC.—A broad distinction must be made here, as well as in actual performance, between the lyric and thematic styles.*

Lyric music is pre-eminently the expression of nature and consequently less formal than thematic music.

With the aid of a few motive figures we can reconstruct almost any composition in thematic style. But when we approach an adagio from Beethoven or Schubert, a cantilena from Rubinstein or Tschaikowsky, or a lyric from Raff or Jensen, we will find few opportunities for applying precepts and formulas. A certain homogeneity in the phrases will be observable, because this quality is a natural product of unified thoughts and moods. This alone will aid us in acquiring mental possession of a pure lyric—that is, so far as the theme is concerned.

With regard to the harmonic accompaniment and the cadences, we can, from our knowledge of such matters, readily supply the accessory parts as soon as we observe the style or form in which the composer desires his picture to be framed.

Period construction by phrases or sections cannot be explained here. That is done in such works as Bussler's

---

* These are explained and illustrated in Theory of Interpretation, Chapters XIX and XX.

Musical Forms, and Complete Music Analysis.   The latter deals particularly with detail and gives many of the forms in diagrams.

The student should understand the usual modes of procedure in period formation, and how the sub-divisions are related to and connected with the complete theme.   A melody from one of Mendelssohn's large works is quoted here:

Scotch Symphony.

The following section is similar, except for the cadence:

The rhythm of (b) is almost identical with that of (a). This element plays an important part ; indeed, the composer must imitate either the rhythmic or the melodic features of his motive in the development of the latter.

But without inquiring too closely into the modus operandi of such themes as the one last quoted, the author is of opinion that their melodic fascination is the surest token by which they may be remembered.   Like a musical voice, a beautiful face, or a gorgeous sunset, the charm of a fine melody ought to produce an instantaneous and indelible impression.   Two or three readings of the theme from Mendelssohn should suffice to enable one to perform it ever after, without notes.

Then, when the motive is developed thematically, our knowledge of its melodic and rhythmic features will enable us readily to grasp the development, for these features constitute the substance of the entire movement.

THEMATIC MUSIC.

This has to a considerable extent been illustrated. The main object here, is to mention the fact that nearly all music in this style can be reproduced, with the aid of a few motives and figures as models.

The instrumental compositions written prior to the advent of Mozart were essentially thematic.

FORMAL OUTLINES.

The single forms; the dance form ; the rondo and the sonata forms, have characteristic outlines which not only reveal their nature to the critical listener, but aid the performer in reproducing and remembering a given form. For instance, the march or the minuet: In Part I there are two periods, usually repeated. Part II also contains two periods, but in a different key, contrasting with Part I. Then, in order to end in the original key, there is a *da capo* to Part I, the repeats being omitted. See the Minuet in Beethoven's Op. 22. (Part II is usually misnamed " trio.")

Suppose the rondo " La Matinee," is selected for a lesson. The form must be well understood in advance, because this will assist us in comprehending the piece as a whole and in knowing, *a priori*, the order in which the different divisions succeed one another. After a few measures of prelude the main theme begins in *D, piano,* and is repeated *forte*—sixteen measures. An intermezzo follows (there is rather too much of this tonic and dominant filigree work), and this terminates with a simple cadenza leading to a repetition of the main theme, exactly as at first.

The second subject in *G,* is about the same in length as the first division in *D*. Another cadenza here occurs in order to modulate back to *D*. Then the principal subject, intermezzo and repetition come again as they did in the first division. The rondo ends with a coda in form of recollection, and a short stretto founded on the figure of the prelude.

This synopsis of the formal outlines applies to very many of the rondos of that "classic" epoch in which the composer, Dussek, lived.

The recurring principal theme, interspersed with intermezzi (interludes), and generally the contrasting second subject followed by the main theme, are the leading features of all rondos.

After mastering the regular themes, the intermezzo and the cadenza, it will be necessary to understand the form, because that shows the order in which the different periods follow one another. Indeed, this knowledge is of great assistance in learning an opus which is written in any of the recognized forms. These should be studied until they are clearly understood, and it would be well to make diagrams of the principal forms. (See the author's Complete Music Analysis, pp. 81, 86.) This is as essential as map-drawing is in the study of geography. Begin with the sonatinas of Beethoven, Kuhlau, Reinecke, Loeschhorn, Seiss. Nearly all of these will contain three independent movements: The allegro, usually exemplifying what is called the sonata form or sonata movement; the andante or adagio, a ballad or other single form, and the rondo form as finale.

ANTIPHONAL PHRASES.

Where two phrases or motives represent thesis and antithesis there is little to guide us in forecasting the antithesis, or response. But the two phrases combined form a design which can be reproduced in any interval suggested by the composer.

A quotation from Beethoven is given :

Ex. 124.

The responses (b) and (d) correspond ; so do the initial semi-phrases (theses), (a) and (c). It would therefore be an easy matter to continue in this style.

The application is illustrated in the following :

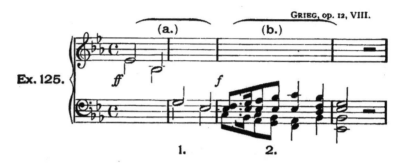

Ex. 125.

GRIEG, op. 12, VIII.

The antiphonal phrase (b) requires more attention than does the thesis (a). This form of complete cadence is to be analyzed so thoroughly that it can be played without notes in any key. The melody begins on the second of the scale and ascends to the sixth ; the bass consists of the same notes read backward—from the sixth it descends to the second of the scale.

Now play the section without notes, *andante.*

Measures five and six are the same as (a) transposed to *G minor*, a diatonic third above. Perform this.

The concluding phrase is not so simple ; but since it is a regular transposition of (b), adapted to the key of *G minor*, no difficulty should be experienced in transferring the design to a parallel key. Follow the harmonic minor scale of *G.*

LESSON XVIII.

MISCELLANEOUS EXAMPLES FROM BEETHOVEN.

The following designs are to be continued, mostly in the free style:

Ex. 126.

(a.)   (b.)

Every phrase of the bass solo commences upon the minor sixth of that particular key, whether the tonic be minor or major. From the indication given it is apparent that each new tonic is a major second lower, and that the figure passes through the dominant ninth chord, the ninth being minor. Examine the phrase and imagine the continuation. Do not play it until the scheme appears plainly in its harmonic as well as melodic aspects.

The third phrase returns to *A flat*, and the sequence terminates there. If it is desirable to complete the period, this phrase may be added:

(d.)

7.   8.

The accompaniment above is to be added in this style:

1.

Ex. 127.

At the end of each phrase there is a natural resolution to the tonic. The two notes above, which at first form the root and third of the new tonic (last half of measure two), continue in alternate reiteration, and become fifth and seventh of the dominant seventh (or dominant ninth) chord. Compare *D* and *F* with the broken chord below, first phrase. The second phrase begins at (b), Ex. 126.   This form of accompaniment continues six measures, then the period is to be concluded with a complete cadence in *A flat major.*

Rehearse the right hand part separately, following the trend of the theme below.   Then the parts may be combined. Repeat until it can be performed *allegro.*

In the transpositions another voice-part is to be added, according to the original :

Ex. 128.

Since the leading note does not appear below, it is included above for the sake of completeness.   This occurs only at the end of each phrase.

In the next quotation a repeated period is outlined.   The sequences are not regular, and therefore the theme is indicated throughout.   But the principal. task consists in carrying out the design of the accompaniment :

Ex. 129.

The design in the bass is regular as far as +. There the triad on *C* is not used, because it would dissonate unnecessarily with the *A flat* above. Hence 1, 3, 6, is substituted for 1, 3, 5, on *C*. Passing chromatics are partially indicated at third and fifth measures. See the ♮.

A perfect cadence is to be used at the close, then repeat. When mastered, the period is to be performed *prestissimo*.

The following melodic sequences should be played fluently after a brief examination of the design :

Ex. 130.

This is not altogether strict, but it is perfectly symmetrical and regular. The model at (a) is therefore sufficient.

The subsequent variant is not so simple :

Ex. 131.

Before attempting the actual performance there are several points to be considered : 1. The harmonic outline is the same as in Ex. 130. That is, four inverted triads succeed one another in this position :

2. The two first notes in each right hand group form an inverted anschlag (see Ex. 65); consequently the related tone comes last. In the left hand groups the first note is an appoggiatura; the other two are related, or harmonic notes. 3. The appoggiatura in every instance is a minor second below the following harmonic note. 4. The sequence descends diatonically, that is, the harmonic outline is diatonic.

When these points have been referred to the example for comparison, the passage may be played.

The following are to be continued as indicated :

The chords are all in the same position, but some thought will be required in order to tell where the chromatics are to be included.

The design at (b), which is a continuation, ascending, of the previous passage, will occasion no embarrassment. After repeating, play the entire nine or ten measures allegro.

Ex. 133 is an inversion :

The model (a) is to be followed at (b), (c) and (d). Compose this mentally; then play it several times until no notes are required.

The accompaniment can be added while the theme below is being sounded; slow at first, then allegro.

Transpose to *D minor*.

LESSON XIX.

BRAVURA MUSIC—MODERN FIGURATIONS.

We will now examine the structure of a few *morceaux* composed since the death of Beethoven and Schubert. The preceding lessons will find application here.

The first selection is "Cascade du Chaudron" from F. Bendel's "Am Genfer See." There are nearly fourteen pages developed from this simple motive :

The first four pages are introductory, the style being *quasi fantasia.* A suggestive chord figuration falls to the right hand. This is mostly simple in design. At the eighth measure the theme is left incomplete and this is merged into a short cadenza. This consists of two dominant seventh chords in alternate succession. They are a minor second apart—an unusual and discordant progression. The cascade figuration in sixteenth notes is continued almost incessantly. The cadenza is to be analyzed, because it appears again in another key.

From measure seventeen there is a transposed repetition of the preceding. While the right hand executes a series of trills (from measure 31 to 44) the left hand plays the motive in isolated forms :

Then there is a measured cadenza of eight measures founded upon this augmented sixth chord:

The figures ascend two octaves, passing through the four positions of the discord. A mere glance at the design is sufficient to enable one to perform the entire ninety-six notes impromptu. This is followed by a series of major chords descending chromatically, 53 to 58, slightly altered during 59 and 60. From 64 to 67 the motive again appears, accompanied by an inverted gruppetto figure; 68 to 71 is a short cadenza on the augmented dominant triad, all the figures being the same. Here ends the introduction.

From 72 (meno mosso) the complete theme is heard for the first time. This should be observed until it can be played without notes; then repeat it, adding a simple chord accompaniment. It will then be a simple matter to include the figuration as indicated, most of these having appeared in the introductory part.

A brief cadenza intervenes, and then the theme is repeated (97 to 116) literally—the two pages being almost exactly alike. From 121 the theme appears below with the figurations above. At 129 (piu vivace) a middle part occurs. The previous rhythms are maintained here; in fact, the new theme is very cleverly developed from the principal motive. (The affinity should be recognized by the student.) Owing to the repetitions this is comparatively simple. The same melodic idea is continued in *A*. The figurations in small notes are appendixes, and should be understood in this light:

These inverted gruppetti woven around the fifth of the tonic chord (and the root of the dominant seventh chord) become easy of execution soon as their structure is apprehended. So we pass on beyond these eleven measures in *A*.

The figure at 155 is twice repeated, each time an octave higher at 156 and 157. Another cadenza commences at 155, and it should be observed that the original motive appears below. The chromatic passage, 161 to 165, is similar to the cadenza from Tausig (Ex. 75), though one descends while the other ascends.

From 167 the theme in *G flat* is repeated with a different accompaniment, and the part in *A* is continued in sequence, modulating back to *B flat*. The intermezzo from 194 is a brief development of the leading motive in fantasy style, easy to analyze and easy to remember. At 210 the complete theme in *B flat* (as at the first *meno mosso*) recurs. From 235 to 250 there is a passage of broken chords, and at 251 the coda begins. The motive is only slightly varied and the figurations are similar. The form is rather peculiar, and this should be particularly observed as it will assist one in retaining the music after the actual notes have been mastered.

From this and the preceding lessons it is apparent that every musical composition admits some form of analysis which tends to reveal the design or mode of construction. From the beginning the author has endeavored to furnish the student a key which would enable him to reproduce a considerable portion of any given passage, or of a complete work. In this way a great deal of time (always valuable to those who realize that it never can be recalled) is economized ; and furthermore, music thus mastered is more firmly retained than would be the case if only the memory, without the understanding, had been exercised. In the matter of sight reading the advantages of this system are almost as great. All the facts and features of music which might assist one in quickly mastering any composition have not been mentioned. To do so would require several volumes. But the way to success has been indicated, and a key has been furnished which will unfasten many locks and bolts and bars.

Sometimes the design of the accompaniment, or of the counter-subject, will furnish a valuable clew. Thus in Grieg's Op. 6, II, there is a melodic design in the bass which is characteristic. This is so natural and progressive that it serves as a complement to the theme above:

Ex. 135.

The scheme occurs several times, and when once observed it is easily remembered, or rather, it is not easily forgotten.

Attention is now directed to the right hand part. In the third measure the melody is the same as in the first measure. But the fourth measure is a sequence of the second, carried a third higher. In other words, the second phrase is constructed by means of repetition and sequence, as often happens.

Sometimes a sequence embraces an entire section containing two motives. Ex. 125 is an instance. There are four measures divided into two parts, thesis and antithesis, in *E flat*. This antiphonal section of four measures is then repeated in *G minor*. This form of sequence is not uncommon, but it can scarcely be classed among the elementary or regular species.

There are numerous compositions whose principal charm lies in the melodic figurations rather than in simple melodic outlines. In such instances the detail is of first importance on account of the absence of pure lyric melody.   While this fact must be clearly understood by the performer the analysis of such designs presents no additional difficulty.   Every elaboration must rest upon some harmonic basis, and this should be understood apart from the ornamentation in order to simplify the task of learning the composition.   The famous etude by Kullak (book II, No. 7 of the Octave Studies) is selected as an example of detail work.*   The two first measures are founded upon the common chord of *E flat* elaborated by means of passing notes, diatonic and chromatic, but in the absence of a lyric theme the melodic figurations become very prominent, as here :

Ex. 136.

In the second measure the chromatic passing notes below are interspersed with the tonic chord, the whole forming an instrumental melodic design.   This is repeated in interrupted sequence form.   Therefore when the first phrase is sufficiently understood the remaining fourteen measures of this part ought to be speedily mastered.   The *meno allegro* contains several melodic outlines, the elaboration being a double trill employing the tone below the principal tone, and without conclusion. The principal harmonic scheme may be seen here :

There are a few chromatic scale passages in alternate octaves followed by under-tone trills, and these conclude the second part.

The left hand executes most of the figurations in that part titled *piu mosso*. The passing notes here, as in the first strain, form an equal part of the design, and are not to be considered as mere adventitious ornamentation.

. Having mentally assimilated the various designs it will be necessary to consider the form, which is quite symmetrical. The first part embraces two pages in the tonic. The second part, *meno allegro*, is the same in length. Part III, *piu mosso*, is technically the second subject. This also occupies two pages, but it is in the dominant. Then the first part recurs and is somewhat curtailed. Part II comes again almost identically, and the second subject is repeated in the tonic. This is followed by a brilliant termination with the figuration of part I as motive. This sketch of the form should be well understood, because it will serve to show the order in which one part follows another and the relationship of the whole.

A brief indication is sufficient to enable the performer to understand all such cadenzas and passages as the following:

Ex. 137.

Each hand executes a series of minor sixths descending chromatically nearly three octaves. Therefore the sixty-eight double notes ought to be played from the indication in Ex. 137. Then there is a brief passing chord figure and the main theme recurs. In this "Rigoletto" fantasia there are several cadenzas and figurations which can be thus reproduced with equal facility soon as their structure is understood.

COMPENDIUM.

GRADES I AND II:

The Music Box, W. Fink, Op. 179, No. IV; Little Scherzo, W. C. E. Seebœck; A Little Melody, Oliver Ong; "I Am Coming," said the Springtime, Ong; The Spinning Room, F. Behr, Op. 575, No. XIII; The Brownies Dance, F. J. Zeisberg; Summer, Lichner.

GRADES II½ AND III:

Danse Florentine, Op. 238, I. Lack; Rondo Brillante, B. Wolff, Op. 151; Old Folk's Dance, Zeisberg; Half on Wings, Zeisberg; Polka Study (I), Zeisberg; Fairy Voices, R. Eilenberg, Op. 115. Da Capo—Stacato Study, Op. 5, F. Heink. Valses Sentimentales, E. Jambor, Op. 4, I. Sunset, W. O. Forsyth, Op. 14, II. The Barn Dance, Op. 10, III, Max Liebling; The Straw Ride, Op. 10, IV, Max Liebling. Tulip, H. Lichner. Rose, Lichner. Barcarolle, H. C. Brainard. The Butterfly and the Rose, F. Behr, (scale figures in sequence, and 3 notes against 2). Hilarity, Lichner, Op. 150, II. Will o' the Wisp, Jungmann. Will o' the Wisp, Seeboeck. Canon, J. Lewis Browne. Tarantella, Jas. H. Rogers. The Mill, Jensen. The Shepherd Boy, L. I. Strickland.

GRADES III½ AND IV:

Selected Studies, D. Steibelt, revised by Wilson G. Smith, (useful for the study of sequence designs, as well as for technic). Polonaise, M. Moszkowski, Op. 18, V. Spinning, J. L. Browne, Op. 12, I. "Lullalo," (an Irish lullaby), W. C. Barron. Sweet Recollections, Aug. W. Hoffman. Bourrèe, Constance Mills, Op. 10, I. Sous les Soules, F. Thome. Capriccietto, Ph. Scharwenka. Buy a Broom, Wm. H. Sherwood. Butterflies, Arthur Nevin, Op. 11, II. Chaconne, A. Durand, Op. 6 2, (composed entirely of natural sequences and repetitions). Serenade Orientale, W. G. Smith, Op. 94, I. A Serenade, H. Brockway, Op. 28. Minuet a l' Antico, No. 3, Seeboeck. Minuet (from the last E flat symphony), Mozart. Minuet in G. (a la Mozart), I. J. Paderewski. Berceuse, Frank Sawyer. Loure, Bach-Heinze. Scherzo, Bargiel, Op. 31. Toccato, J. L. Browne, Tempo di Menuetto, Ph. Scharwenka. Teresita's Waltz, Carreno. Caprice Romantique, R. C. Jackson.

GRADES IV AND V:

2nd Mazurka in G Minor, Saint-Saëns, Op. 24, II. Allemande (from Suite), E. d' Albert. Walter's Prize Song, Wagner-Bendel. Valse Gracile, H. W. Parker, Op. 49, III. At Home, E. Nevin, Op. 30, IV. Valse Dansante, J. H. Rogers. Valse Noble, H. Carri, Op. 31. Papillons, Grieg, Op. 43, I. 2nd Valse, B. Godard, Op. 50. Troika (sleigh ride), Tschaikowsky, Op. 37, XI. Tarantelle, Chaminade, Op. 35. Spring Song, Emil Liebling, Op. 33.

GRADES V AND VI:

Etude Melodique, Op. 118, C. Chaminade. Song of the Brook, Lack. Valse Noble, Op. 102, II, L. Schytte. Barcarolle in G., Rubinstein. Pas des Amphores, Chaminade, Op. 37, I. Valse Romantique, Chaminade, Op. 115. Witches' Dance, Mac Dowell. Waltz, Op. 64, III, Chopin. Bridal Song, Op. 45, Jensen-Lassen. Valse Brillante, Op. 23, Blumenschein.

GRADES VI AND VII:

If I Were a Bird, Henselt, Op. 2, VI. Magic Fire Scene, Wagner-Brassin. Mélodie Plaintive, H. N. Bartlett, Op. 124. Spinning Song from The Flying Dutchman, Wagner-Liszt.

Made in the USA
Middletown, DE
15 March 2016